GET SPORTY

Netball

Edward Way

WAYLAND

Published in 2013 by Wayland

Copyright © Wayland 2013

Wayland
338 Euston Road
London NW1 3BH

Wayland Australia
Level 17/207 Kent Street
Sydney NSW 2000

Editor: Nicola Edwards
Designer: www.rawshock.co.uk

The author and publisher would like
to thank Broadstone Hall Primary
School and Epiphany, Shanice, Josh,
Elliot, Lauren, Amy, Hannah, Lucy,
Elliot and James for their help with the
photographs for this book.

British Library Cataloguing in
Publication Data
Way, Edward

Netball. -- (Get sporty)
1. Netball--Juvenile literature.
I. Title II. Series
796.3'24-dc22

ISBN: 978 0 7502 7168 4

Picture acknowledgements

All photographs by Clive Gifford apart
from p13 Hannah Johnston/Getty
Images; p15 Hannah Johnston/Getty
Images; p19 Phil Walter/Getty Images;
p21 Hannah Johnston/Getty Images;
p27 Quinn Rooney/Getty Images.

Printed in China.

Wayland is a division of Hachette
Children's Books, an Hachette UK
company.
www.hachette.co.uk

CONTENTS

PLAY NETBALL!

Netball is an exciting, fast-moving team sport. Mostly it is played by girls, but boys can play netball too. Two teams of seven players try to pass and move a netball around a court. The aim is to score more goals than the other team. In a full game, which lasts 60 minutes, over 100 goals can sometimes be scored.

PLAYING THE GAME

Players cannot run with the netball. They must pass it to team-mates.

1 A game of netball begins with a centre pass. This is made by a player called the Centre from a small circle in the middle of the court.

2 The team with the ball attacks, moving it around from player to player and aiming to get the ball forward towards the goal.

3 Attackers must be able to catch the ball at all different heights and pass it accurately. Defenders try to stop attackers from passing or shooting and aim to gain control of the ball.

4 Each team is allowed two players inside the shooting circle, a semi-circle surrounding the goal. The Goal Shooter and Goal Attack are the only players allowed to shoot at goal.

5 This attacker has caught the ball, turned, and is taking a shot. The defender stands tall to try to block the shot.

6 For a goal to be scored, the ball must travel down through the hoop fitted to the top of the goalpost.

7 Goal! A quick celebration, then players get back into position fast. Each team takes turns to restart the game with another pass from the centre circle.

GET STARTED

Netball players wear a t-shirt or vest and shorts or a skirt. Every player on a team wears the same colours.

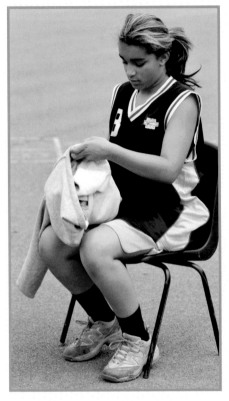

A sweatshirt or a tracksuit will help to keep you warm before and after games.

Your trainers need to fit well, support your ankles and offer plenty of grip. Make sure your laces are tied tightly. Cotton sports socks protect your feet from blisters and absorb sweat.

When playing as a team, you wear the same coloured bib as your team-mates. The bibs are printed with letters showing each playing position (GK is for Goalkeeper).

THE BALL

Netballs have a rough or pimpled surface to offer grip. Older children and adults play with a size 5 netball. Younger children play with a size 4 ball.

THE COURT

Position	Allowed in court areas
Goalkeeper (GK)	1, 2
Goal Defence (GD)	1, 2, 3
Wing Defence (WD)	2, 3
Centre (C)	2, 3, 4
Wing Attack (WA)	3, 4
Goal Attack (GA)	3, 4, 5
Goal Shooter (GS)	4, 5

This Wing Attack is offside as she has stepped into the shooting circle. The referee will give the ball to the other team. This is called a free pass.

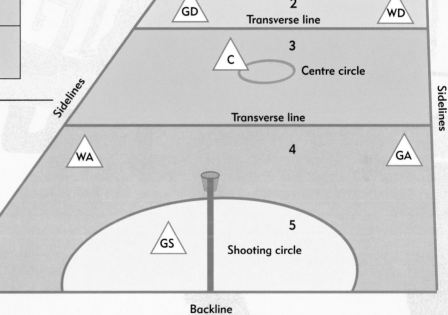

When the ball bounces outside the sides of the court, the team that did not touch it last takes a throw-in. The thrower stands outside the sideline and passes the ball back into play.

JUNIOR NETBALL

Younger players can play a five-a-side version of netball, such as High Five or Netta. Games are played on a full-sized netball court but the rules are a little simpler and players are given more time and space to pass and shoot.

PLAYING FIVE-A-SIDE

The five playing positions on court are Centre, Goal Defence, Goalkeeper, Goal Attack and Goal Shooter. Players can only play in certain areas.

The Centre can play in all of the netball court except the two shooting circles.

The Goal Attack and Goal Shooter can play on all the court except the shooting circle their team is defending.

The Goal Defence and Goalkeeper can play everywhere except the shooting circle their team is attacking.

SIMILARITIES AND DIFFERENCES

Five-a-side netball is much like the full game but it does have some important differences. You do not play the whole game in one position. All players get to switch places.

1 In five-a-side and regular netball, you are not allowed to throw the ball so far that it crosses both horizontal lines across the court. If this happens, the umpire awards the other team a free pass.

2 Just as in regular netball, players have to leap high or lunge low to try to catch the ball.

3 Players have four seconds to pass the ball after catching it in High Five. In Netta, they have up to six seconds.

4 The goal is 41cm lower than in full netball (65 cm lower in Netta) to give younger players a better chance to shoot.

5 In High Five, a defender is allowed to defend a shot. In Netta, defenders must step away and let the shooter shoot.

UMPIRES AND RULES

Netball matches are run by officials called umpires. They make decisions about the rules and whether players have broken them.

PENALTY!

Netball is a non-contact sport. If serious contact is made, the umpire will award a penalty pass. The team that was fouled is given the ball and can pass it without a defender in the way. For other less serious offences, the opposing team receives a free pass. When a free pass is taken, a defender can stand in position as for a regular pass.

TOP TIP

Always follow the rules of netball. Giving away a silly penalty pass or free pass can spoil your team's chances.

FOUL!

Holding, pushing or wrestling an opponent who is trying to catch the ball is serious contact.

If you pass the ball while sitting or kneeling, the umpire will award a free pass to the other team.

You cannot kick the ball at any time. If you do, the other team will be given a free pass.

When you pass the ball it has to travel through the air. If you just hand it to a team-mate, the other team will receive a free pass.

THE TOSS UP

Sometimes, two players may wrestle for the ball at the same time. The umpire will signal a toss up.

1 The two players face each other at least 0.9m apart. The umpire stands between them.

2 The umpire throws the ball into the air. The players jump to compete for the ball.

3 Play continues after one player has control of the ball.

THE UMPIRE'S SIGNALS

Umpires use hand signals to show their decisions to players. This umpire is signalling (from left to right) a toss up, a goal scored and a time out, which is a break in play.

CATCH IT!

Catching is a crucial skill in netball. A player making a good catch gets the ball under control quickly, ready for a pass or a shot.

A SKILFUL MOVE

Try to use both hands to make a catch and be prepared to lean, twist and bend to reach the ball if it is wide or low. You must be on your feet and not sitting or kneeling when you catch the ball.

1 Keep your eye on the ball and the thrower as you get ready to make a catch. Spread your fingers out wide to make a big W shape.

2 Stretch your hands out in front of you to meet the ball. Keep watching it all the time.

3 As you make the catch, bring your hands into your chest to cushion the ball. Aim to make an immediate pass.

HIGH CATCHES

To make a high catch, watch the ball and time your jump carefully. Spring upwards and extend your arms to meet the ball. Grip its sides and bring your arms quickly towards your chest. Bend your knees to make a cushioned landing.

TOP TIP

Practise your catching as often as you can. You could work with a team-mate to throw the ball at different heights and angles.

PRO PLAY

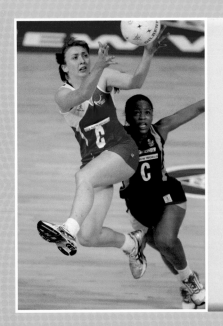

Top players learn to control the ball in the air. You are allowed to pat the ball once in the air to control it before catching, but no more than once.

PASS IT!

Players use different ways of passing the ball to move it around the court. The chest pass is the most common. The shoulder pass is used for longer passes.

TIMING AND ACCURACY

The aim of good passing is to send the ball at a speed and height that makes it easy for your team-mate to catch. You are only allowed up to three seconds to pass the ball, so you must decide quickly which player you're going to pass to and which pass you're going to use.

THE CHEST PASS

1 To make a chest pass, spread your hands around the back and sides of the ball. Bring it up to your chest with your elbows bent. Focus on where you want to send the ball.

2 Straighten your arms to push the ball away. It should leave your hands with a flick of your wrists and fingers. Follow through so that your arms point in the direction of your target.

To use the chest pass over longer distances, you must move your weight forwards into the pass. Straighten your arms strongly and flick the ball away powerfully.

THE SHOULDER PASS

1 Gripping the ball securely, bring it up to just above the height of your shoulder.

2 Push the ball forward from your shoulder in the direction of your target. Release the ball with a flick of your wrist and fingers just as your arm straightens.

TOP TIP Practise your passing as often as you can. A good practice is to pass two balls quickly between three players standing close together. Keep catching and passing the ball as quickly and smoothly as possible.

PRO PLAY

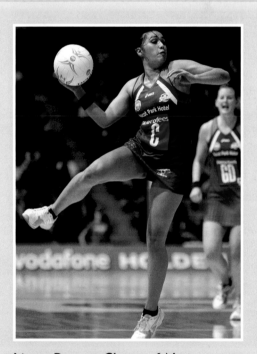

Liana Barrett-Chase of New Zealand is ready to make a powerful shoulder pass. She has identified a team-mate who is in a good position to receive the pass.

HIGH AND LOW

Often you'll have to pass the ball when an opponent is in the way. Using either a high overhead pass or a low bounce pass are two ways of moving the ball past a defender to one of your team-mates, the receiver.

TOP TIP As soon as you catch the ball, you should be looking to make a good pass. Sometimes, you may be able to pretend to pass in one way, then quickly make a different pass.

THE BOUNCE PASS

1 Bend your knees, get low and lean to one side of the defender. Hold the ball securely.

2 Push the ball downwards from your chest. Aim for a spot on the ground behind the defender.

3 Release the ball with a flick of the fingers. It should bounce a little over halfway between you and your receiver.

4 The ball should reach your team-mate between waist and knee height.

THE OVERHEAD PASS

Grip the ball in both hands and lift it above your head. Aim between your team-mate's head and chest to make it easier for the receiver to catch the ball.

Swing your arms forward from the shoulders and release the ball with a firm flick of your wrists.

PASSING PRACTICE

Your coach will show you different ways to practise your passing. One is to play two attackers v two defenders in a small area marked out with cones. The two players with the ball try to complete as many passes as possible while staying inside the area. If the ball leaves the area or is intercepted by the two defenders, the pairs of players swap jobs.

TOP TIP If your receiver is on the move, aim the ball a little ahead of them so that they can run onto the ball.

PIVOT!

Once you have caught the ball, you can pivot to change direction before you pass it.

SWIVEL AND STEP

You pivot by swiveling around on one foot and taking steps with the other. The swiveling foot is called the pivot foot. It must stay in the same place or the other team will be given a free pass.

2 Keep your upper body still as you pivot. Look around the court for a chance to make a good pass.

3 As long as your pivot foot doesn't move, you can make as many steps as you like with your free foot. Remember, though, you only have three seconds to release the ball.

1 This player's left foot is her pivot foot. She can swivel on it as she takes one or more steps with her right foot.

When you catch the ball in the air, the first foot that touches the ground is called your landing foot. You can pivot using your landing foot or you can lift it to take a step. You must let go of the ball before your landing foot touches the ground again.

PRO PLAY

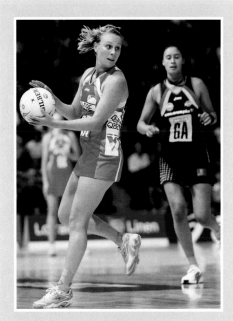

Australian netball star, Vanessa Ware shows how top players scan the court looking for an opportunity to pass as she turns on her pivot foot.

GET FREE

You can pivot to turn away from an opponent, leaving you free to make a pass.

1-3 This attacker is being marked closely by a tall defender. She turns on the ball of her right foot and takes several pivot steps with her left foot.

4 Seeing a team-mate free to her left, she turns and passes. Part of her pivot foot must stay on the ground until the ball has left her hands.

MOVE AROUND

Moving around the court well will give your team-mates with the ball good chances to pass to you.

GETTING FREE

To get free of opponents who are marking you (see page 24), you need to use changes of direction and speed. You can also try to convince them that you are moving one way, only for you to move the other way.

1 You can lean in one direction, then push off hard and sprint in a different direction.

2 Sprint as hard as you can, keeping your head up to look for a pass from a team-mate.

3 As soon as you are free, move your hands up and out ready to receive a quick pass.

TOP TIP Be realistic about how far your team-mates can throw the ball to you. Don't run into space that is too far away for a pass to reach you.

THE ONE-TWO PASS

You can cut out a defender by playing a one-two pass.

1 This player passes the ball to a team-mate and then sprints hard into space.

2 The player who catches the ball turns at the waist or pivots using her feet.

3 She quickly sends a pass just ahead of her team-mate for her to run onto the ball and catch it.

TOP TIP

If you are not passed the ball, move out of the space you have run into – it is valuable! A team-mate can then try to enter that space.

If you get free but are not passed the ball, don't stop. You can sometimes change direction and still stay free of your opponent.

PRO PLAY

Australia's Julie Pendergast moves quickly and at full stretch to challenge Adine Wilson of New Zealand for the ball during the final of the 2007 Netball World Championship.

SHOOT!

The only way to score points in netball is to shoot the ball through the hooped goal at the top of the post. Shooting needs a good eye and steady nerves.

SHOOTING TECHNIQUE

Before you take your shot, get your body and the ball in a straight line with the hoop.

1 Lift the ball, holding it on your fingers, not the palm of your hand. Steady the ball with your other hand.

2 Your shot starts from your legs upwards. Bend your knees and keep your back straight throughout as you take the shot.

3 Straighten your legs and, as you rise, stretch your arms upwards. Aim the ball above the hoop.

4 Send the ball away with a flick of your fingertips. Your hands and arms follow through a short way in the direction of the hoop.

UNDER PRESSURE

In matches, you will shoot with a defender in front of you. Defenders will make themselves as tall as possible and hope to block your shot or put you off. Keep focusing on the rim of the net and send the ball high out of the defender's reach.

TOP TIP

Once you have taken your shot, stay alert and move into a good position in case the ball bounces off the hoop or the post and stays on the court.

PRACTISE AND IMPROVE

Practise your shooting as often as you can, taking shots from various positions inside the shooting circle. This helps you to learn how much force to use to send the ball different distances.

You could have a shooting competition with a friend and see how many shots out of 20 each of you can score.

As you improve your technique, you can start shooting with the ball held high above your head.

DEFEND!

When your team loses the ball, you are defending. All seven players on a team must try to defend well.

MARKING

Defenders try to stop their opponents getting into space to receive the ball. They cannot push, hold or touch them, but they can stand close to them and move as they move. This is called marking.

1 A Goal Defence marks a Goal Attack inside the shooting circle. He stands in front of his opponent to deny her an easy chance to get the ball.

3 As the opponent moves, the Goal Defence moves and leans in the same direction. He tries to block a pass.

2 The Goal Defence has to turn his head to see where his opponent is moving.

TOP TIP When you are defending against the player with the ball, you are allowed to stand close, but no closer than 0.9m away.

KEEP MOVING

You need to stay active and alert when marking the player with the ball.

1 Lift your arms up and out to make it harder for your opponent to make the pass.

2 If your opponent twists at the waist or pivots round, turn with them.

BE READY TO INTERCEPT!

By making an interception you can win the ball back for your team.

1 This Goal Defence has spotted a high pass made by the other team. She times her jump to reach the ball first.

2 She stretches high and gets her hands onto the ball just ahead of her opponent.

3 As she lands, she pulls the ball to one side away from her opponent. Now she will look for the chance to make a good pass.

TOP TIP If the player you are marking gets free from you, sprint hard to get back close to them.

IN THE SHOOTING CIRCLE

The two shooting circles are where attackers score goals and defenders stop goals being scored. They are the places on the court where a game is won or lost.

ATTACK AND DEFENCE

Only two players from each team are allowed inside a shooting circle. The Goalkeeper and Goal Defence try to stop the Goal Attack and Goal Shooter from scoring goals.

1 A pass is made into the shooting circle. Both defenders and attackers run towards it.

2 The Goal Attack has reacted sharply and looks the likeliest player to catch the ball.

3 The Goal Defence cannot get two hands to the ball to catch it. But she can reach out with one hand to knock the ball away and stop the pass.

1 The two defenders mark the two attackers closely. They aim to stop them getting into space, as this would give them time to catch the ball easily.

The shooting circle defenders both mark Australian shooter Kristen Hughes. This is called double teaming. The shooter must stay calm and focus on making a good shot.

2 The Goal Attack and Goal Shooter try to time their sprints and dodging moves to get free. Here both attackers have got ahead of the defenders.

TOP TIP If the ball is loose in the shooting circle, try to pounce on it quickly. You may be able to lean over the goal line to catch the ball before it bounces out of the court.

MAKING THE TEAM

Netball is a fast, athletic sport so you need to be really fit to play at your best. Working hard on your skills will give you a better chance of being picked to play for your team.

TRAIN HARD

You can practise some skills, such as shooting, on your own or with just a couple of friends. Training sessions with your whole team are the best way to learn attacking and defending moves. Turn up to every session and listen to advice from your coach.

BALL HANDLING GAMES

Here are some drills you can do to help improve your flexibility and ball handling skills.

1 Stand with your backs to each other. Pass the ball back over your head to the other player and then bend at the waist low to receive the ball between your legs. Do this ten times before switching direction with your team-mate.

2 In another version of the drill you twist at the waist to pass the ball to your team-mate then twist back to receive the ball on the other side.

TOP TIP You'll work hard in a training session or match, so make sure you take plenty of sips of water during breaks.

PREPARE WELL

Before a game or training session, players get their bodies and minds ready for action with a warm-up.

1 This often involves some jogging…

2 …and other vigorous movements, such as star jumps, which get the blood pumping round the body and make the muscles warmer.

3 You need to stretch your main arm, leg and body muscles before playing. This helps reduce the chance of muscle injuries. This player is stretching his upper thigh muscle.

4 Your coach can teach you a good range of stretches. These players are stretching their shoulder and upper arm muscles.

GLOSSARY

attackers
Players in the team that have control of the ball.

centre circle
The circle in the middle of a netball court from which a game starts.

coach
An adult in charge of a team and its training.

court
The area on which a game of netball is played.

defenders
Players in the team that try to gain control of the ball from attackers.

free pass
A decision by the umpire to give the ball to one team when the other has performed a foul or broken the rules in some way.

interception
When a defender manages to catch the ball during a pass between players in the other team.

marking
Staying close to a player from the attacking team to deny them time and space to receive the ball.

offside
When players move outside the areas of the court in which they are allowed to play.

pivoting
Turning around on one foot when you have the ball in your hands.

receiver
A player who catches a pass from a team-mate.

shooting circle
The semi circle surrounding the goalpost inside which shots can be taken.

throw-in
A way of restarting the game when the ball bounces out of the sides of the court.

time out
A break in play ordered by the umpire or asked for by a team.

toss up
A way of restarting the game when the umpire is unable to award the ball to either side.

umpires
Officials in charge of running a netball game and making sure that everyone plays by the rules.

warm-up
To perform some exercises before a game to prepare your body for the effort you'll need to do well.

RESOURCES

BOOKS

Sporting Skills: *Netball*, Clive Gifford, Wayland, 2007
For slightly older readers, this book uses step by step photography and diagrams to get into the techniques and tactics of netball.

Starting Sport: *Netball*, Rebecca Hunter, Franklin Watts, 2006
A simple guide to learning to play the sport.

101 Youth Netball Drills (Age 7-11), Chris and Anna Sheryn, A & C Black, 2010
A collection of drills, exercises and games to improve your netball skills.

WEBSITES

http://news.bbc.co.uk/sport1/hi/other_sports/netball/default.stm
The BBC's netball pages contain news of top matches but also include videos and tips on techniques like passing and shooting.

http://www.englandnetball.co.uk/youth/
The youth section of England Netball's website has a fanzone, skills videos, a gallery and much more besides.

http://www.netball.asn.au/extra.asp?id=783
A good summary of the rules of the sport can be found at the Netball Australia website which also has news of teams and players in action.

There's a lot to learn when you start out playing netball. Most important of all is to remember to have fun! Netball is great fun to learn as part of a team. If you have not played before, why not round up some friends so that together you can all…Get Sporty!

INDEX